CLIENTS & CASES

By

David S. Brannon, J.D.

ISBN-13: 978-0615660288

Foreword

This is the book I wish I could have read on my first day as a lawyer. Nothing in this work was taught in law school. Everything was learned in a courtroom. It is my hope that this book can save you some stress.

CLIENTS

The real challenge in the practice of law is dealing with the clients. What the client may have done may be a challenge; who the client is will be a challenge. As you begin your initial contact with your client, pause for a moment and reflect on the fact that your potential client needs something they cannot provide for themselves, in this case legal representation. How does it feel, not wanting something but needing something?

Empathize with the person who is in need. If this individual is acting oddly, or aggressively, or is depressed and withdrawn, consider how you might act in their situation. Are you at your best when in need? Any potential client should want to show their attorney the best they have at this first meeting. Is that what you get?

Whatever behavior this person demonstrates is probably going to turn out to be their best life coping skill. Recall this display of limitation as the case unfolds. Recall it when you find yourself asking if your client is in touch with reality. Recall it when you ask how much they are involved in their own life. Clients often have willful blindness in regards to their mess. It may be the one life skill they have in abundance.

A line I use a lot with clients is "let's not pretend." Clients do not like it. No one likes being told they are wrong. People want to hear that they are in the right. Pretending the facts are other than they are will not carry the day. Fantasy will fail in the face of unbiased testimony.

Good lawyers learn patience with odd and inappropriate behaviors because they understand that fear is the driving force behind that behavior. Displaying patience and forbearance is your first step in accomplishing your first task with any new client. That first task is to earn the client's trust. Both client and attorney "win" when the client trusts the attorney. Both need that trust. Both want that trust to develop. It can happen, but it takes work on the part of the attorney.

EARNING TRUST

A good place to start thinking about trust is, how did you meet this new / potential client? Was it an arms-length transaction? Did each of you choose to work together? If so, then you have crossed, successfully, the initial trust threshold. If the client, after shopping around, "bought" *you*, your starting position is strong. Don't get smug. You have to keep winning that trust over and over. And, maybe you were just the low bid?

Nothing in the legal arena happens quickly. As the case drags on you will have to re-justify that trust decision made by your client. You may have to re-do it many times. Criminal or civil, legal proceedings are difficult, unpleasant experiences. Many people live their entire lives and never have the shadow of the legal system block their sun. Your client was not that lucky. Your client will need to hear "buck-up" from time to time, coach. You can only help with that if the client trusts you.

You hold yourself out as knowing the way through a dark, scary place. You can't, won't and don't promise any specific result. That's because you are honest. You do promise to be diligent, attentive and responsive. That's because you are a professional. Add in your "x" factor and, from your point of view this client has every reason to place their faith in you.

If you are court appointed you became counsel of record without an "okay" from the person you represent. Why should this person trust you? For heaven's sake this person is not even paying you. Who should the person think you work for? Many appointed clients hold it against their appointed counsel that they, the client, cannot afford to hire an attorney of their own choosing. When you encounter this attitude recognize it but don't let it get you annoyed.

It would improve the dynamic between the client and attorney if, at that first face to face meeting, the client reached in their pocket, took out one dollar and gave it to the attorney. That simple and financially insignificant act would get the client invested in his representation.

Otherwise, from the client's point of view the legal advice he gets costs nothing, so that's what it's worth --- nothing. Even a single dollar moving from the client's hand to counsel would improve the entire experience for the client, as well as shoring up the client's self-esteem which tends to be low. After the case is over the client will be assessed attorney fees which will get reduced to an unsatisfied civil judgment. This is not the same thing as paying your own way up front. Clients are thoroughly surprised by the assessment even though they've been told it's going to happen.

Having met you your appointed client faces their first big test, and it concerns YOU! Your client must decide,

Can I, Should I, Will I, Do I TRUST THIS LAWYER?

When your client trusts you they do not blame their fear on you. If they trust you they believe you are doing what you can, when you can, to help them. Their trust in you helps them to survive this tempestuous experience. The client who trusts their lawyer is better able to manage their own stress level.

If the client does not, cannot, or will not trust the appointed attorney the stress that creates hurts both client and counsel. This makes the creation of any genuine attorney-client confidence unlikely. Clients need someone to trust in this situation. Do they trust you?

If the client does not trust counsel then, and despite what it says on a piece of paper in the court file, this client is alone. Alone goes hand-in-hand with afraid. The simple reason it is so important to earn or win the trust of your client is because your CLIENT IS AFRAID. In this job we deal with fear all the time. We will look at the role of fear a bit later. But know that if your client is being ruled by fear then your client is capable of doing themselves lots and lots of damage.

The things you do to earn and keep trust turn out to be relatively easy. Return phone calls, especially with family members who speak daily with the client. The client likes the fact that you take the time to speak with his mother, father, sister, when they call. You want to give your client's family members a reason to speak well of you.

Send your client a note when things are slow and nothing has happened for a while. The critical issue is the timing of these events. It's not so much what you do as it is when you do it. Timely, and even better, snappy response can win trust. And, while the client evaluates you, you have the chance to take his measure. The more you understand your client, the better it is for you.

When anyone is forced to rely on someone else to provide what they cannot provide for themselves it is a recipe for stress and fear. Needing a doctor, dentist, mortician, attorney – none of these bode well for the customer. Reflect on this as you contemplate what it means to serve as a professional for a person in need. In your mind what you bring to the table is education, experience, judgment and discrimination. You think that's a lot.

Your client expects magic and will swear on a stack of Bibles that magic is what you promised. The danger that you may fall short of magic is part of why your client is afraid. At mental and emotional levels the client knows you can't perform magic. That frightens your client. After all, your client knows the true facts of the case in a way you do not and never will.

So, start getting on top of your client's fear while trying to fathom who your client is. And, while you are at it, win your client's trust. That process starts with the first interview. Whether you know a lot about the case or next to nothing, I suggest you allow the client to believe you know nothing about their situation. Clients want to write on a clean slate. So let them do so.

EXCEPT THAT I DON'T.

THE FIRST HERESY: DO NOT LET YOUR CLIENT TELL THEIR STORY

Your client may be about to explode with the desire to tell their story. At the beginning of your representation you don't want to hear it. You can talk football, food, girls, whatever, but at this juncture don't let the client relate anything they are going to assert is a fact. You are stuck with any "fact" that comes from the client's mouth. That is true whether that "fact" turns out to be true, helpful or something else. The better practice is to NOT let your client get stuck with anything until it cannot be avoided.

In the criminal arena the burden of making the case rests on the State. Let them carry their burden. Learn the facts as you will face them in a trial. Once you grasp what is going on in the case you can present the OTHER SIDE'S CASE AGAINST YOUR CLIENT TO YOUR CLIENT. Lay out, in language your client understands, the case against them. It is at this point you can allow the client to respond if they wish to do so. A majority of the facts are usually NOT in dispute. Right away you start paring things down to the essentials of the case. Where the client's story diverges from the State's story is where you seek your trial issue.

If, at this point, your client speaks about their case, pay attention to what the client thinks is important. Compare how the client wants to see the case with what you see through the lens of the State's evidence. Those stories won't line up exactly, and where the misfit occurs will expose what the client thinks is important, probably pointing the way to your issue.

Working your case this way gives you the advantage of seeing the other side's facts and deciding -- for yourself, without the client's input -- if the State has a case or not. This is how you learn about your client. How your client reacts helps you judge the strength of your client's proposed defense or explanation or rationalization. Can you see a makeable case that your client is guilty? Can you articulate a defense?

Some clients balk at having to wait to tell you their truth about what happened. In an effort to keep the client quiet while you learn the case, ask your client if they have ever played cards for money. When they say "yes" ask if they had the chance to see everyone else's cards before they decided what to bet, if deciding to bet at all. When their reply is "no," ask if they would like to play the game that way. They will say, "of course." Learning and understanding the State's case before making any decisions about what to do is like playing cards where you get to see the other gamblers' cards while they are not allowed to see yours. Then you decide what to do. Clients understand this explanation.

This approach lets you get comfortable with the case against your client before attempting to incorporate the client's take on things. Just now THE CLIENT'S VERSION IS NOT REALLY IMPORTANT despite the client's insistence that if the prosecutor would *just listen* then this case could be dismissed. In a criminal case what the State alleges drives the ship. Just now the State's thinking is what we seek to understand.

While awaiting discovery spend more time learning about the person you represent and less time worrying with the case. Between being appointed or retained and receiving your first pile of discovery materials the law is not going to change. You either already know the relevant law or you will by the time you need it. The facts are what they are and not subject to change, just interpretation. As the case unfolds you will grasp how the facts interact and the story plays. Early on focus on winning your client's trust. That prize makes whatever comes next easier (on you).

STILL WORKING TO EARN TRUST

Shortly after your first face-to-face meeting, especially if the client is in the county jail (which provides limited choices in entertainment), you can expect to receive

An urgent phone call – the client must see you, now!

Respond very quickly. Even if it is incredibly inconvenient at that particular moment, go see the client. Here's why:

It is unlikely that anything substantive has changed in the case. Translated: your client probably does not need to see you. The client is mulling over whether or not you can be trusted. With few resources to call upon there is one way your client can test your sincerity and commitment to their case – they can ask to see you. By the time your client does this you may be certain they have heard those around them complaining about how they never see their attorney, who never comes to speak with them, and obviously does not care about their case. Your client does not expect to see you.

So, show up, and do it now. Don't be too surprised when your client is confused, sometimes seriously confused, as to why you are there. They called you? But they see your face, so we're done here. When the client sees you their worry about ever seeing you calms down. *The more certain the client is that they can reach you, the less they feel the need to do so.* The less they fear, the less they call. Especially early in your involvement, take those calls that come from the jail, and leave some time for quick visits. There's a genuine return on those investments for you.

A quick response can earn a trust point. Trust points are very valuable. Earn and bank all you can on your client's behalf.

Tell clients that they won't see you very much, especially in the early hours of the case. As discovery arrives they can expect to see a lot of you. Then, when the case goes to trial, you can promise that your client will see you way more than they want to.

TRUST CAN BE ABUSED

CAVEAT: After that initial visit, then the urgent phone call with its' accompanying visit, the client's next call / demand is problematic. It is coming. It gets a quick response, but pay attention to the reason behind the call. Is the client's need real or imagined? If the call / request is about something real, anything legitimate from the client's point of view – the client hears from family about what is said on the street and thinks you should know; the client remembers something a cop said that seemed strange and thinks you should know; someone in jail is trying to talk about the client's case and the client thinks you should know -- all is well. But far more likely the client is going to say, "what's going on?"

If that happens re-give the "at first you won't see me much . . ." speech. Explain that you are busy with someone else's case, that when the client's case gets hot the client will get all your attention. Stress how, if something, anything of importance happens, you will be there as quick as you can.

Watch that you do not become the client's plaything. You do one trick – you show up, and your client is really, really bored. Come and do that trick for your client's amusement!

Don't perform tricks on command. While you must be sensitive to legitimate concerns of the client, does the client really need to see you? Are they just bored? This "attorney as plaything" is especially likely with the client who has been confined for long periods of time. The jail strips from residents all control over their own life. The residents can still do one thing – they can call you. So they do.

Some of the people in custody can fairly be described as conmen and women, or more generically "grifters." This is a person who gets through life by taking advantage of the good nature and naiveté of the people around them. Lawyers, who are by nature helpful, can easily get pulled into this client-scam. It is not personal. This person, your client, does this with everyone they meet. What any person can do for "me" is this client's only concern. It's their best life skill.

Many clients try and scam you for whatever they can get. You will know they have done so when you find yourself putting your money in someone's jail canteen account. It happens. Pay attention.

When you realize your client is trying to scam you, bust them for it. Don't confront with aggression, but ask your client, with a smile, "Do you really want a lawyer you can fool?" You will enjoy the look on their face. Your client will like the fact that they can't play you.

When the jail is their whole world clients learn to function there. Your presence reminds them that trouble is waiting. Those confined for long periods prior to some resolution of their case often hide from their possible fate. When the attorney shows up, hiding is no longer possible. That's a stressful event for most clients. Seeing their attorney is often not a happy event for the client.

WHO PLACED THE CALL?

Very early in your representation someone from the clients' world is going to call you. Take that call. Learn this person's name and get their numbers and email. The first person to reach out on behalf of the client is an important player in your client's life. Make a friend of this person. This early caller's impression of you and your work will matter to your client. *Your client trusts this caller.* You want the client to trust you, too. While your client is debating whether or not to trust you, the opinion of this person is going to carry weight. Give this first caller a reason to take up your cause.

Invest some time with this person. The fact that they care enough about your client to call makes them important to you. Even if only on the phone (paying attention that you don't reveal anything confidential), keep this person in the loop. When this caller gives good reports on you to your client it encourages the client to place their trust in you. It's another chance to win a trust point. Trust points get traded in when the client has to make some hard choices. Never miss a chance to bank a trust point.

It's worth mentioning here that whatever you say to this important caller is going to be repeated to your client when client and caller speak later. Be aware that any conversation over the jail phone system is recorded. What someone says you said may, probably will, be heard by your prosecutor. Pay attention to what you say on the phone. Important things should be said in person, attorney to client, face to face. What gets transmitted by phone is confidence and hope.

JAIL CALLS ARE NOT SECURE

Any call into or out of the jail is recorded. Letters you send end up where? Letters can be time bombs. Neither of these routes of communication can be considered secure. Important things should be related, in person, attorney to client, and face to face.

Right now your client is waiting for you to return and lay out the case against them, and hopefully, explain how you might defeat that case. How this gets done is in the section titled "Cases."

ABOUT CLIENTS

CLIENTS GET LITERAL – WATCH YOUR (and their) WORDS

Clients get literal with the words in their case, whether spoken aloud or in a document. If the charging instrument says "the client made a hand-to-hand sale to a buyer in a blue car," but the car was actually red, in client-algebra this equals "I am not guilty."

Clients grasp at any straw to claim "not guilty." Pay close attention when speaking with your client. Watch how they parse the words in documents and those you speak. Even the client who wants to trust the attorney is wary of being too open. For many clients this is a well learned life-lesson.

When your client discusses their case pay attention not only to what they say but to how they say it, the specific words they use. Make sure you speak English and not legalese. Translate the case into your client's version of English. For impact you may, occasionally, swear. Never reveal you are afraid of the case or where it may lead.

The words your client speaks are important. The words they do not use may be important, too.

When a story is proceeding along, and then suddenly veers off, something is being avoided. That is a place to return to in your interview and to ask more questions. Your client will answer your questions. Your client wants to answer your questions. Just watch how they do it.

A simple example – your client is telling you about a walk they took, and the story is being related one city block at a time. Suddenly the story jumps six blocks and ends. Why the jump? Maybe it means something, maybe it means nothing. But that sudden gap is a place for you to fill with follow-up questions.

Clients often stick as close to what happened as they can, veering away from the truth only when their own culpability – as the client imagines it -- emerges. Watch for those sudden veers. That's where you usually find the issue in your case. Clients routinely confess to the crime without realizing it. Client's really should just shut up.

WHAT CLIENTS GET TO DECIDE

The client gets to make two decisions in a case: (1) whether they will plead guilty or not guilty, and (2) if at trial, will they testify? This is the sum of what the client gets to decide. The counsel of record makes all other decisions.

Your client does not need to know this. It often upsets clients to hear this. Whose life is in the balance, anyway? Remember the jailed client is bored to death, and arguing with their attorney is more fun that sitting in a cell. For your client, arguing with you feels like they are doing something to help their situation.

Keep your client informed about what is happening. Ask their input on as much as you can. Let them help as much as they can. It is the client's life, after all. But remember which two things the client decides, and who makes the rest of the decisions. Your decisions are based on trying to achieve the client's goals, whatever they may be. You have been down this road before and your client, hopefully, has not. Let your client think they are making all the decisions; that's okay. Remember whose case it is.

Use letters and visits to keep the client aware of your efforts. Your letters may be the only respite the client gets from the monotony of the jail. You probably won't hear a thank you. If you needed that you would not be doing this work. While you are doing all this to keep your client up-to-date, know that hearing from you does not necessarily make your client happy. What's a lawyer to do?

FLAMING YOUR OWN CLIENT

You do not have to like all of your clients. You probably won't like them all and that's okay as long as you still work hard on their behalf.

There are going to be days when all you want to do is leave your client to their own devices allowing them to crash and burn. Many clients are hell-bound to damage their own case in any way they can and there are day's on which you would gladly let them. When you really want to skin your own client, consider: You can't do this difficult job if you are angry. It helps no one and hurts everyone, especially the attorney.

Lawyering is a toxic profession. Most lawyers don't grasp how this job can and will damage them. Good lawyers realize that nasty feelings directed towards their client indicate a loss of equilibrium on the part of the attorney. It's time to get away for at least a weekend.

There are going to be cases where you like your client as a person. There will be other cases in which you receive your client with less warmth. You are under no obligation to like your client. Your responsibility is to help your client, not to be their friend.

Here's a tool to add to your quiver of life skills: Whenever unsure of whether you should speak certain words to your client, ask yourself (1) are these words true, (2) is it necessary that they be spoken, and (3) will speaking them be an act of kindness?

As long as you get three "yesses," you may speak. This is a useful censor to install. The desire to burn your own client is a good indicator that you, yourself, have fried-up. It is vital to be able to recognize when this has happened.

"We call it the justice system, but really, it's just a system" – Raleigh attorney Howard Kurtz

ACCEPTING THE SYSTEM

The rules of the criminal justice system are structured to capture – and it is fair to say, exploit – human nature. There is a human need, or desire, or drive to speak in the aftermath of an emotionally charged event. Committing a crime is often an emotionally charged event, especially if the perpetrator is a novice at such behavior. People who have committed a crime want to talk about what went down. The closer in time to the event, the more wrenching the event, the stronger is the drive to speak. That is why police are so aggressive about speaking with people as near in time to the criminal act as is possible. They know the perpetrator they seek will speak to someone so strong is this drive. The perpetrator is often willing to speak to a police officer, as amazing as that sounds. Very few clients do the thing they are advised to do by that same police officer, which is to shut up.

Make peace with the rules of the system. The law could be that "police cannot speak to a suspect without an attorney present." That could be the rule, but that is not the rule. Our system is structured to admit whatever first comes out of the mouth of any suspect. The system believes that those early statements tend to be close to the truth. Experience demonstrates that what gets said will be instructive if not dispositive. The statement might get labeled "spontaneous," or "against interest," but whatever it gets called if the words came out of the mouth of the accused – your client -- you can rely on facing them at trial.

And, yes, your client spoke after being arrested. You know he did. He spoke after being advised to be quiet. You know he did.

The better option for the client would be to shut up. Most perpetrators can't do it. Most non-perpetrators can't do it, either. In the emotionally charged post-crime state of mind perpetrators are primed to speak. They want to explain. They want to strut. Police know this and are trained to pay close attention to those first words. The criminal justice system depends on this dynamic acting out. Any accused is primed to do maximum damage to their case and any potential defense with little or no prompting.

All this happens before you, the attorney of record, ever get to the case. And all this happens after the person has been told, by a person wearing a uniform, that they have a right to (1) shut up and (2) can speak to a lawyer, and (3) can think before they speak. Clients happily waive all three rights.

We are often delivered to a confession that "I was there but he did it." It might help if high school civics taught a chapter on accomplice liability. Would that help in the face of human nature?

THE FELONY MURDER RULE (I Didn't know I was confessing!)

People charged with crimes quickly develop a deep and profoundly unfounded assurance that they know the law, understand the law, and have done nothing to break the law. This is the awesome power of denial. Some people live with a strong belief that, if a person says "no" long enough and loud enough, it becomes true.

Some clients come through this syndrome and start listening to their attorney. The clients you tend to remember are the ones who never make this crossing. They will argue any point of law with the assurance of a judge in their voice. This person is never going to admit they don't know what they are talking about. They often don't know that fact themselves.

When representing such a person you must be careful to document each step you take in the case, explaining to yourself and to the client, on paper, how each decision is reached. Copy the client with everything relevant but not confidential. Do this through regular letters, written in client-English, explaining where the case was, where it is now, where we might be going next, and, if you know what's around the next bend. Set out for your client how you frame the issue. Tell the client directly, "this is the problem in your case." Without using the term start teaching your client your *theory of his case.*

Practice your theory of the case on your client. Who cares more about your thinking than them? Remember to pay attention how you say what you say. Your client is likely not the only one reading your letters. Your client may read your letter to their family during a (routinely recorded) jail visit. Your client may ask a fellow inmate to explain something in your letter. Your D.A. may hear your letter, too. Anything truly confidential should be discussed face to face in person.

This is a combination of due diligence and CYA. Do not think you are the person who will get through to this client and lead them to understand how life works. This client is often a bar complaint a year or so down the road. When you have a client who will not listen to you, you need lots of detail and care with the case file. Any future discussion you may have about this case will not be for a year or more. Leave bread crumbs to find your way back to understanding why you did what you dd. Then, when the time comes, never be afraid to explain yourself to an appropriate reviewer. It's all part of the job.

YOUR ATTITUDE IS THE KEY

Start with the expectation that your case is going to trial. This point of view does a lot for the attorney. Setting your heart for trial gets you out ahead of the client whining about "his life, man!" Ideas that never crossed the client's mind before facing these charges – his bright future, his beloved family and his pending return to complete his education – become of paramount importance. The client feels stress and the feeling is unpleasant. Your client will happily transfer that unpleasant feeling to you if you will carry it.

Many people do not want to be in control of their own lives. People don't want to think, weigh and consider options. That seems especially true of many criminal defendants. Such defendants often take the attitude that their mess is YOUR fault and YOUR responsibility to fix.

You can't fix these people. You can't make someone take charge of their life, and you can't make a non-thinker into a thinker in the time you have available. The client could, if they would, put the bit in their mouth and pull their own wagon. They seldom want to do this as it takes effort. It's easier just to blame you.

Parallel with this experience is the anger many clients carry against the attorney because the attorney is being paid by the state. That is not the attorney's fault. If any fault is to be assigned it lies with the person who needs, and cannot afford, legal help. Clients will treat you like you are the S.O.B. who has them over a barrel. Many, many clients will say, to your face, that you, their own attorney, work for the D.A. And, if you are not outright working directly for the prosecutor you are at least in cahoots with the State. There is not much you can do about this, so if and when it happens don't let it get under your skin. Remind your client that they are free to retain counsel of their own choosing at any time.

Early on tell your client how proud you are to represent them, how they have a right to their day in court, and how you are looking forward to trying their case. Tell your client that if they do not want a trial – if they want to explore where a plea might lead

– they must say this to you. Your position is that your client's important matter is for trial. If the case is not for trial, if the client wants a plea, they must specifically tell you that.

Be sure to mention your ethical obligation to bring to the client's consideration any plea offer that comes from the D.A. Explain how the law imposes on the attorney duties on behalf of the client. One of these duties may be to carry a plea offer to the client. Deciding what to do with an offer is the client's decision. Remember whose case it is --- that communication from the D.A. is not about you, it's about your client. Even if it makes your client mad, deliver all messages from your prosecutor to your client.

This "going to trial" attitude has power. When your name appears on a file you want the D.A. to think "one more trial!" For a state employee that translates as "more work for the same pay." For the defense counsel for many years (it's changing) going to trial created billable hours. A known willingness to go to trial might improve any plea offer your client receives. That may induce your client to at least "explore" the idea of where a plea might lead.

Another annoying problem "going to trial" addresses and often corrects is the client who states that, at an earlier time, some attorney forced them to accept a plea when they were not guilty. Use a "going to trial" approach and, even if that is said of you, it will not be true.

CLIENT NARCISSIM

The high level of narcissism which many criminal defendants display is a challenge for the attorney. You meet this face to face when you are listening to jail phone calls between your incarcerated client and their loved ones back in the world. You will (or should) receive these recorded phone calls as part of your discovery materials. Use these calls to gauge how self-centered your client is by noticing the first issues they address in that first call. When those first concerns are:

> →Who is my girlfriend seeing, which gets expressed as "sleeping with," or something less polite and
>
> →When are you going to put money in my jail account, and how much?

When these are your client's initial concerns you will know their priority is themselves. Everything is about them, whether they admit this or not. Decisions are about what's best for them and them alone. All the client wants is for you, the attorney, to dismiss these charges and let them go home. If you can't, or won't do that, why does the client even need you?

Don't make more out of this than is justified. A person in jail with no real chance of being granted bond or getting a bond which they can make, is going to be primarily concerned with themselves. It would be unusual for it to be otherwise. Whether they admit it or not, clients know the reality of what they have (allegedly) done and have a good idea what they are up against. You can identify what your client thinks is important, what your client wants to be important, by how your client responds to the uncontroverted facts of the case.

Do not expect the narcissistic client to make any decision based on anything other than what they want. Any matters taken to your client must be presented in the form of what the offer does for the client. My experience has been that nothing less than a clean dismissal of all charges accompanied with a heart-felt apology from the State will satisfy the narcissistic client.

If your analysis reveals that a case can be made against your completely self-absorbed client, and you can't deliver that clean dismissal, you are going to trial. For the narcissistic client who goes to trial and loses, well, that was your fault. If they go to trial and win, see, they told you they did not need a lawyer! For this type of person nothing is ever their fault. It's a tough way to go through life. Remember who you are dealing with and don't let these all-too-common personality types get to you.

SECURITY

Your client in the jail and in possession of their discovery materials can be a disaster waiting to happen. At every opportunity remind your client of this danger. Someone else in confinement may access your client's discovery materials, study them, and then present themselves to the office of the District Attorney as having information about a pending matter. Jail snitches trade on loneliness and fear. Being confined in the jail can be too much for some personalities to bear, and clients become easy marks for a confidence game.

The scam works like this: the soon-to-be-snitch reads your client's materials and tells your client, "this is B.S. You aren't being treated right." This is exactly how your client feels, and now he's being told he's correct. That damn lawyer never tells me this! At the same time the new reader / snitch-to-be calls his own attorney and says, "I've got information. Let's go see the D.A." The D.A. will talk to that person.

Client narcissism makes them vulnerable to sweet words blown in their ears. The more someone tells them how unjust it is that they are locked up at all (which is how your client feels), the more your client will reveal. The more detail the client reveals the better the story the snitch will have for the prosecutor. The snitch will have a level of detail that makes believers of listeners, whether D.A. or jury. There is not much you can do about this. Keep trying to get the client to return the discovery materials to you, for you to hold till this is over. Tell your client that, when this is over and they want this stuff, they can come to the office and pick it up. This seldom is sufficient to hobble the client's tongue, but you do what you can.

The snitch's power comes from telling your client what your client wants to hear. That may be something the client's attorney seldom, if ever, gets to do. If you were locked up which of these two would you prefer to hear from? But try and recover those discovery materials. There may be nothing you can do to stop your client from talking about their case with other inmates, but you can take steps to try and cut down the level of detail available to the snitch.

Every time you see or write to the client, remind them to shut up about their case. They may not do it, but you tried.

Clients are the true challenge of this profession. Without them there is no need for any of us. Use your colleagues as a resource for figuring out how to help you manage difficult personalities. Your client needs you and you need your colleagues. Don't be afraid to ask for their help. Rest assured that a time will come when they will need, and ask for, yours.

# # #

FEAR

Fear is our topic at the center of this work. If that seems odd, consider fear as a primary driving force in life. Lots of people in this world are afraid. When you are involved in someone's legal problem recognize the place of fear in your situation. Fear may be making decisions. It may be bubbling below the surface or it may be spewing violently from your client's behavior, but fear is there.

Why might the players in this legal drama be experiencing fear? What does your client stand to lose? Money, freedom, their life – no reason to worry there. Worry is the red-headed, bastard step-child of fear. Is opposing counsel afraid of something, maybe losing? Do you know opposing counsel's situation? Is their job at risk, maybe through no fault of their own? Did they screw something up recently? Are they fed up and don't care anymore? Did they ever care? Most frightening of all, has this case hit one of their "hot buttons," and their fear is not maximizing your clients' punishment?

Most people, and lawyers are people, hide from their own fear. Many who are driven by fear would deny that fact, to your face, and sincerely believe in that denial. Fear can be subtle. It works effectively by not being recognized.

Clients hide their fear. Young males especially will mask their fear in front of just about everyone. You will become skilled in identifying masked displays of fear. Darting eyes, rapid, shallow breathing, hands shaking uncontrollably are all clues that unseen forces are working. Fear manifests in choice of words, body language and inappropriate flashes of anger. There is a reason behind every act done and undone. Sometimes what does not get said speaks louder than what does get said.

The client who can't get on-board with how his attorney wishes to conduct the case may be signaling that his fear is winning the internal fight with trust. Once you've explained, maybe more than once, why it would be best to do things your way, allowing the attorney time to master the facts, a fearful client may still refuse. This does happen. Go back and resell how you want to do the case and why one more time. Then, if the client still wants to call the shots you must remember whose case it is. Be sure to tell them, "Before we are finished you'll wish you had listened to me. That's because I've been down this road before, and you have not."

There is a good chance that your client does not recognize their own fear. Fear can control from a level below conscious awareness. In this state a person usually does not, probably cannot make good decisions. Fear shapes their landscape. What they imagine coming out of that fear may, or may not, comport with actual reality.

At this juncture your job is to assess if your client is able to see and acknowledge the various facts they need to consider to make informed decisions. Those decisions are theirs to make. You must do your best to make sure your client takes in everything they must. You may need to continue the case so your client can think about things. It is the client's case, and the client who lives with the decisions made. You will try and help your client manage their fear. You may succeed.

What about your fear, counselor? Once upon a time your biggest fear was failing out of law school. That did not happen. Perhaps you next worried about what would happen if you failed the bar exam. That did not happen and now, do you worry about missing something in the case? I hope so, because that would mean you care about this task you have taken on voluntarily. You can use fear to sharpen yourself as well as injure yourself. Whatever can hurt can also help. Are you manifesting task avoidance? That's fear. Why else do you avoid that certain file on your desk, the one covered with the protective layer of dust?

When the fear driving any case turns out to be that of the attorney (YOU), you need to recognize that fact. Quite often acknowledging your fear helps to stop it from calling the shots in your life. Many people find that speaking aloud what they fear, while looking at themselves in a mirror seems to reset their internal, emotional balance. Fear grows stronger when denied. Fear fails when confronted. Some people visualize their fear then see themselves engulfing or consuming that same fear. They visualize themselves absorbing and using the energy contained in their fear. Rather than fleeing from this energy or hiding in denial, it is more productive to take that energy and use it to work the case.

Dealing with fear is a big part of the practice of law. Everyone confronts and deals with fear all the time. That is true of you and of your client. Part of the attorney's job is helping the client cope with their fear in the case. Fear will lock your client up tight, and it is usually better to keep the client loose if that is possible.

The clients' fear can drive them to disaster. Fear keeps them from fairly assessing what they are up against. That can mean a quick trip to a bad result.

Do not tell a frightened person that they are afraid. People hate being told this. Some lash out at the accusation. Many people are afraid of being afraid, a kind of fear that manifests as angry outbursts. If you represent a client who is reacting to their own fear, perhaps you can help them see what is happening in their life. Steer your conversations to that fear-point. Ask your client to reflect on their feelings and thoughts. Yes, some of this is social work or psychobabble, but this may help your client get back on top of the situation. Actually doing something which might help is part of why your job title includes the term "counselor."

Any acknowledgment by your client of their fear tends to lessen the power and influence of that fear. There isn't a formula for this, just a need to confront and defeat this invisible power coming from within.

Sometimes the client turns the fear into energy and does what is required to minimize how much damage they suffer. Those cases make it fun to do this work. It sure ain't the money or the respect.

Working with a client who is defeating fear is exciting. You get to watch a person unfolding into the experience of their life, strange as that experience may seem from your perspective. Most of the world spends life curled up small with eyes tight shut. Being with someone as they unfold and take control of their life is the opposite experience.

WHEN FEAR IS WINNING

More common, unfortunately, is the client who remains locked into their fear. This person cannot see what is going on and is not going to make good decisions about what to do. This is the client who:

Denies it is them in the surveillance photo, or
Insists the policeman is lying, or
Says "no" to everything and holds their breath till blue in the face.

Some clients will not put their hands on the wheel. Will they ever own the things they have done? They may spend years locked up, angry at everyone and everything. They end like this because they want to pretend what their life is about, not recognize their own place in creating their reality. I call this living in the wish world. It is very common.

It all comes from fear. At some point in your case preparation it is useful to identify all the sources of fear in your case. Work through each player --

judge, D.A., defendant and their family, victim and their family -- and the supporters of those players. It is not uncommon for a jailed defendant's decisions to be coming from his mother waiting at home. If that is the case you must understand the mother's fear as well as how her fear impacts what she is telling her child. Go have a cup of coffee with this person. You will learn a lot. That knowledge will be helpful to your client.

For some clients in some cases the best they can do is hide and pretend. It's the wish world, again. When your client chooses this route you, my fine attorney, often become a lightning rod for the client's fear. The simple sight of you means the client can no longer pretend this is all a bad dream. They must, at least while you are in front of them, face a bad reality.

When you find yourself at this point anticipate a lot of aggressive behavior on your client's part. Anger armors their fear. It feels like all that anger is being directed at you -- because it is. You can get pulled into your clients' fear. Resist this. Two frightened people are worse than one frightened person.

You must find the strength to lift yourself above this potential fray. That may be a challenge, as lawyers tend not to walk away from a fight. But if you are reactive to the situation you risk being drawn into the client's fear. This reinforces the walls your client is hiding behind. That is not the zealous advocacy you owe your client. Remember, we want the client's trust.

Understanding the place of fear will help win the trust of your client. Start earning that trust the very first time you and your client see one another. Despite their fear you <u>can</u> win your client's trust. How to win trust is discussed in "Clients." What to do once you have (hopefully) won that trust is discussed in "Cases."

# # #

CASES

The first consideration in any case is how to engage the finder-of-fact. To carry any case you must (1) Draw the attention of your jury by (2) Teaching them just enough evidence so they come to the conclusion that (3) Everything you say is correct.

What delivers you to this goal is having crafted a simple, believable, flows-from-the-facts *THEORY OF THE CASE.* Your theory (1) explains the evidence, (2) frames the issue and then (3) demonstrates why your client is in the right. Now, here's the hard part:

At the time you arrive in the case the facts are what they are,

And the law is what it is.

You will have no impact on either.

You play the cards as dealt.

Do not take this in a fatalistic or negative way. There is a tendency amongst attorneys to spend time trying to gin up evidence that just isn't there. Resist this – it seldom works and really ratchets up your stress hormones. Consider instead paring things down. You are going to spend a year, possibly more, learning a big case prior to trial. Your eventual finder-of-fact will spend only a very few minutes with the case. They will never care about the case the way you do. Except for their obligations with <u>this</u> trial your jury does not care about your facts at all. Trouble is you want them to care. Getting the jury to care is the function of the *theory of the case*.

Developing a theory of the case takes some time and effort. You shoulder this work with but one aim – to make you, the attorney, *CREDIBLE* in the eyes of the jury. There is no way to overstress how important it is to be the credible advocate – the one seeking the truth – in the eyes of your jury. This becomes crucial when your adversary is clearly out for blood. In a close case *YOUR CREDIBILITY* may be what tips the scales in favor of your client.

Nothing is as important – for you and your client – as you being regarded as credible by the jury. An attorney working with a jury has nothing on which to trade except credibility. You may do brilliant research, have a gift for trial tactics, or be a natural with legal theory, but if you don't come across as credible your practice will be sad and so will you. Whether or not you are perceived as credible is all up to you. So is the more important question of whether you are actually credible or not.

NO CASE OR CLIENT IS WORTH THE SACRAFICE OF YOUR CREDIBILITY

You earn credibility with your jury by demonstrating a comfortable, reasoned familiarity with your facts. Your presentation is not strident. You start with a deep breath and slow things down. Your deep familiarity with the facts allows you to discuss your case starting from anywhere in the narrative and ending with your client on top. What makes this possible is having a well-crafted, simple *theory of the case.*

Your theory is a simple story covering as few facts as required to (1) address the important evidence and (2) frame the issue and (3) demonstrate why your client should prevail.

EVERY CASE HAS A THEORY. You do not have to develop the theory in every case. Most cases resolve rather quickly. But anytime you have a possible trial, start casting your nets for information which will allow you to assemble the theory. Even when your expectation is that the case will resolve without a trial, there is value in developing your theory of the case. Having a theory with which you are comfortable gives you the ability to:

Speak comfortably about your case with the court, and

Speak comfortably about your case with opposing counsel, and

Help keep your client focused on what he's up against, and

Make answering questions about the case a comfortable task.

A *theory of the case* comes into being like this:

Gather any and all facts you may be up against at trial. At this point in the process everything you learn is information. Some of this information may become evidence later. Evidence comes in a courtroom from a witness stand. But, for the moment, take in everything you can from any <u>source open to and known by your opponent.</u>

Before you hear the first fact you already know a great deal about the case. You know who has what burden of proof. You know what the other side will need to make its' prima facie case. What evidence will the other side need based on the allegations? What is the source of that evidence? Is it believable? Is it admissible? As you begin the task seems huge, but don't give in to fear. Just take the first step. Start crafting your *theory of the case*.

Do your best to TAKE NOTHING FROM YOUR CLIENT. The "why" of this we have discussed in "Clients." There are numerous heresies in this work and this is one. You don't want your client's story. Not yet, anyway.

As you begin gathering information be open to whatever you find. As you start the process just accept what is there; you will judge later. Say this is your pile of facts after you get things organized:

> This crime occurs late at night in a modern apartment complex, with a disproportionally large Hispanic population and lots of extended families in residence. It is warm on the night in question and lots of people are milling about visiting and passing the evening with friends and family. One family, consisting of Mom, Dad and sister, live in a ground floor unit. On the night in question people are milling about.
>
> There is a knock at the apartment door. When the door is opened a 300 pound, black male, bald with a full beard, is standing there. The visitor asks after someone by name. The person being sought is a friend of the father who resides in the apartment. The person being sought happens to be sitting in

the apartment living room, in a chair and visible from the front door. The large b/m at the door sees the person he wants and calls this person to step outside with him.

When the man in the apartment refuses to accompany him, the large b/m at the door pushes his way into the room. The two men wrestle in the chair then fall to the floor, their struggle continuing. The large b/m draws a gun, and as the fight continues the gun discharges.

The commotion has drawn sister from a back bedroom. She steps out as the gun discharges and sister is struck in the head. Mom starts screaming and rushes towards her child, when a second shot is fired. Mom is struck and collapses on the floor. The large b/m flees and police are called.

The large b/m is later arrested in the company of two other black males. All three are charged with murder under the felony murder rule. No weapons are ever found or tied to this crime. Ballistics indicates that each victim is struck with a different caliber of projectile. Sister dies and Mom survives.

Once you have this bulk information use it to prepare a LIST OF THE UNCONTROVERTED FACTS. *An uncontroverted fact is a detail of the case your finder-of-fact is going to believe is true.* Whatever that fact is will be true for the jury. At this moment your task is to be that reasonable juror. You need to see these facts as your eventual jury will see them. Do your client some good and see what is in front of you, not what your client, or you, might wish were there.

Your list of uncontroverted facts may be as short as (1) a dead body on the ground, and (2) your client is in the area. Or your list may turn out to be long and detailed. It varies case-to-case. The *theory of the case* you finally articulate MUST NOT, AND WILL NOT DENY ANY OF THESE UNCONTROVERTED FACTS. These are "true facts."

You create the list as you work to assemble, *without the client's input*, a short story that makes sense and has no loose ends. The tale may be long or short, but as you grasp the facts <u>as a juror will,</u> a simple story emerges. The story is logical and rolls off the tongue with ease. The words flow when you fit the facts. Don't decide ahead of time what the story says. Let the facts speak honestly to you. You want to experience, as will your jury, the simple story told by those facts. Have the jury's experience before the jury does.

Gather all information, engage your common sense and ask, what makes sense? Uncontroverted facts are the stepping stones of truth. Once you can identify the jury's "true facts," you will have an outline for both your opening and closing statements. Both these statements will make extensive use of these uncontroverted facts. The list of uncontroverted facts shows you the lay of the land in your case. The uncontroverted facts must become back-of-the-hand familiar to you.

I keep using the term "uncontroverted facts." You know the jury is going to believe something. You must know which hard facts will emerge which your jury is going to believe. Regardless of what those facts turn out to be, and maybe, especially, if those facts hurt your case, you must be aware that they are coming. You never want to learn something new while in trial. Strangely, you almost always do.

Accept the uncontroverted facts as truth. Do not deny the facts on your list. Your list is the truth because that is what your jury is going to believe.

Your uncontroverted facts may lead to the inescapable conclusion that your client is in trouble. More on this later. For now don't be concerned about what the facts say. Just boil it all down to as simple a story as you can, as long as it is the complete story. 100 words are good; 50 words are better; 25 words are golden.

Hypothetically:

IF you know from your list of uncontroverted facts that you must admit your client is present at the scene of the crime, then you grasp that the alibi defense offered by your client is . . . in error. If you know the client's presence will be an uncontroverted fact for your jury, it is an uncontroverted fact for you, too. Denying what the jury believes to be true is a fast track to failure. Clients avoid this reality at their own risk and peril.

If it is an uncontroverted fact that the client is present then the client must not, himself or through counsel, deny his presence. The jury will interpret any such denial to be a lie told by the client. Lies invite conviction. If the client is present, he's there. If he's been charged with a crime your job is to explain how that happened and show how those charges are not true. Jurors know police make errors, but you must show how the error occurred to overcome the presumption of "guilty if charged." When a client denies something the jury believes to be true the jury is happy to convict and go home. Don't ever lose sight of what's on your list of uncontroverted facts.

If, by your list of uncontroverted facts, you know your client is present, and you deny his presence, that damages YOUR credibility. This is why it is crucial to identify the uncontroverted facts. Liars deny facts. Liars get convicted. As hard as it may make things, if your client was there, admit that fact and shift the discussion to "why" he was there. Can you say "mere presence rule?"

As part of your case preparation you must make decisions about which facts are so clearly established and fundamental that you can be certain your jurors will accept them. This is not hard to do. These decisions get made in both brain and gut. Is your emerging theory of the case a simple story that makes sense? Test your growing understanding of how the facts function in your case by questioning / challenging your thinking with family and friends [soon you will have neither]. Test your thinking on people whose minds are not impaired by a legal education. Just like the members of your jury.

Do not deny anything on your list of uncontroverted facts. To do so invites maximum punishment. As long as your finder-of-fact sees that you agree with them as to what belongs on that list you will be perceived as smart, honest and insightful. As quickly as you deny anything on that list you are a lair, and worse, a lying lawyer. Arguing with uncontroverted facts, even if you do so at the top of your lungs, is not the zealous advocacy you owe your client.

Do you play Sudoku? In that game certain blocks are already filled in as play begins. You can't change them. You must take on the puzzle with those numbers already placed on the game board. Are those numbers obstacles or clues? Crafting a theory of the case is much like this. Uncontroverted facts are either obstacles or clues. Learn to approach them with gratitude.

Accepting the uncontroverted facts allows you to speak with the jury about facts the jurors are going to believe. You believe in those facts because the jury believes in them. When you speak about these facts you are speaking the truth before the jury. The jury agrees with you, and that can't hurt.

Speaking truth allows you to speak with assurance. You will not say something the jury believes is an error, or worse, a deliberate misstatement. You mirror the jury's perception of truth. Using your theory of the case allows you to repeat a short, coherent story from the start of the trial to the conclusion. The jury will be treated to your theory many times. Your story is built as much as possible out of facts the jury believes are true. You do not want a dispute with the jury. You want to be credible in their eyes.

Return to your example and pull the uncontroverted facts out of the pile of information you gathered:

> A family consisting of Mom, Dad, and sister live together in an apartment. There is a knock at the door one night after the sun has set. The door opens to reveal a 300 pound black male, tall, bald with a full beard standing at the door. The man at the door inquires about a friend of the father, and then sees the person he seeks sitting in a chair in the living room of the house. He calls for this person to step outside, and is rebuffed.
>
> The large man pushes his way into the apartment, drawing a gun. The two men wrestle on the floor. A gun discharges. A bullet strikes and kills sister. A second shot rings out and Mom falls, but will not die from her injuries. The large man who came in flees. Police are called.
>
> Ballistics concludes that two different calibers of weapons are discharged in the apartment.

This shorter story pares out of the original mountain of detail. *This shorter story is the truth for our jury*. The purpose of this effort is to find the bedrock facts of the case. You want to identify facts that you are certain the jury will include when it crafts its' version of the story. It is doubtful that many, or any, or these uncontroverted facts will come in the form of testimony of an interested witness. Should that be the case, remember George Kelly's admonition:

"Assume Everyone Is Lying"

As the case unfolds you will discover who was or is speaking the truth. But that axiom helps you build on facts which will not be rejected by jurors. *Establish as much of the case as you can on independently provable facts; preferably provided by the other side's evidence.* If you wish to add a fact to your list, and that fact is coming from a potentially biased witness – someone who cares how the case comes out – ask yourself, why? Is this biased witness the only source of this uncontroverted fact? If so, are you sure this is an uncontroverted fact? Biased witnesses can give truthful testimony. Just try not to count on them if you can help it.

FINDING THE ISSUE IN YOUR CASE

This list of uncontroverted facts will help you distinguish what is and is not the issue in your case. Identifying the issue is your next big step in this process. When you are satisfied that you have articulated all the uncontroverted facts of the case it is time to articulate the issue of the case. You find the issue by walking up and down your list of uncontroverted facts and asking "how does this make my client guilty?" *The issue of the case revolves around why anyone would believe your client did anything wrong.*

It is quite likely that your list of uncontroverted facts has delivered you to a big hole in the story. That hole will be located around the question of your client's responsibility for this crime. That "hole" is the issue in your case. You must express this hole in the form of a question. How the question gets asked is important. How the question gets asked helps steer how it gets answered. How it gets answered determines what happens to your client.

Here, then, is your next step – IDENTIFYING THE ISSUE in our case.

[New Heresy] SHOCKER: Lots of talented and successful lawyers disagree with this assertion, but every case reduces down to one (1) issue, one question. You must be the party that phrases that question and sells the jury that "this" is what the case is about. *You want the answer to your question to be found in the evidence provided by the other side.* Making YOUR case from THEIR evidence is strong. Is it strong enough to carry the case?

Return to our example and you can see that the issue in the case is, "who fired the second gun?"

Now, answer the question you ask. You want the answer to come from information provided by the other side. That may impact the choice of words you will use when phrasing your issue question. In our example, begin with the uncontroverted facts: who is without a doubt on the scene? How likely is it that each of these people has a gun? Work through each person who is on the scene questioning each as a candidate for the second gunman/woman. Will your jury allow that such-and-such a person has the second gun?

Consider how you will present your issue / phrase your question to your jury. Words will work, but is there an image that might do the job better? Finding a bridge between your issue and the jury's life experience will be better yet. Does your issue impact a common life experience that most jurors will have had? Can you find one potential juror who has "adopted" your issue in voir dire? Watch for a chance to give your theory an advocate in the jury room during deliberations.

You learned to articulate your list of uncontroverted facts. Now you must articulate the central issue in the form of a question. Frame that question to steer the jury to your preferred answer.

Cases may have many small issues but turn on a single, central issue. That crucial central issue is the one you must identify. How that issue gets framed and interpreted determines guilt or innocence. That is why identifying the issue of your case is critical. You must state for your jury, as simply as you can, the issue of the case – what the case is about. Say to your jury, "The question for you to answer is . . . ."

If you don't set out the issue of the case the other side might. If you can't coherently state your issue, who can? The words you choose steer how the issue is presented. It is not uncommon to be the only advocate setting out a complete package – facts, issues, and theory for the jury. Your organization gives you the chance to present a strong position – your theory of the case.

Frame your issue as a question. Frame the question so that the answer works to your client's benefit. Combine the issue and the list into a story about how your client got charged and why the charge is not true (at least beyond a reasonable doubt). That story is your *theory of the case.* Your emerging theory will go through multiple edits as the story sorts itself out. Boil it down; get it tight. 100 words are good; 50 are better; 25 are golden.

Your eventual job will be to teach / sell your theory to the jury. The jury can and will do this work themselves. However, if the work is offered already done, *and seems fair*, most juries are happy to ratify someone else's version of the facts. But to do that they will need to find the person giving them a shortcut to be CREDIBLE. Jurors are people and people will cut corners if they can. But they must believe they are doing the right thing,

Show the jury that their work is done and need only be voted on. Your opening and closing statements are a sales pitch for your theory. Having a *theory of the case* now informs each and every decision you have to make at trial.

THEORY OF THE CASE AT WORK

A theory provides a litmus test for what to ask, or not ask, any witness. "What can this particular witness do to bolster my theory?" is the operant question? Allow each and every witness to do whatever they can to help sell any or all of your theory to the jury. If a witness can't help you sell your story, ask no questions.

QUESTION WITNESSES WHO CAN BOLSTER YOUR THEORY OF THE CASE. As much as you can you use the other side's evidence to tell, and sell, your theory of the case. Use THEIR evidence and witnesses to demonstrate YOUR story. If a witness can add even one thing, let them do it. If they cannot, say "no questions." There is no requirement or etiquette that you question each witness. If opposing counsel makes a production out of questioning each witness in a pro forma style, declining to join that game may win your client some sympathy with the jury. Additionally, speaking less can make what you do say carry more weight, assuming you actually have something to say.

The uncontroverted facts list, your articulated issue and your evolving *theory of the case* help you stay on the facts and avoid sewing confusion when addressing judge, jury or opposing counsel. You say things you know the other guys believe. Because you agree with them to your jury you seem both wise and honest. Your words agree with the listeners thoughts because you rest your efforts on your list of uncontroverted facts.

The list also teaches you what NOT to say. You will not deny the truth represented by your list. You will not argue against what is on the list. Even if the client wants you to. Maybe especially if the client wants you to.

Using a *theory of the case* helps get the facts organized in your head. That organization allows you to relax when speaking about the case. The facts make sense to you. You see how the story flows. You grasp the facts as a flow of events. Things that make sense are easier to remember. Your theory of the case makes sense.

You are learning to walk comfortably with your facts. Your comfort will allow you to enter your story at any point, discuss anything you find, and wrap up with the reason why your client should prevail. This familiarity with the facts, and your obvious comfort when speaking about those facts, makes you CREDIBLE in the eyes of your jury. Your voice is calm and relaxed. You betray no stress. Any stress in your voice will be picked up by someone on your jury and conveyed to any who missed it. Any stress on your part gets interpreted as YOUR DOUBT about what you are saying. Doubt is not good.

Acknowledge each uncontroverted fact, each stepping stone of truth, with your jury. In deliberations the jury will discover that you agree with them about so many of the facts in the case. They like that about you.

Up to now nothing you are working with has come from your client. Your list of uncontroverted facts emerged from the evidence which you know will be used and relied upon by the other side of the case. You learned all this information in discovery. All of your facts come from the information used by the other side, making those facts virtually unimpeachable. When so much of your case flows from facts presented by the other party, how can that party object to where their own evidence leads? If you only say things the jury believes are true – your list of uncontroverted facts – the jury thinks you are smart and honest, just like them. Tell your story with their evidence. The test of your advocacy comes when you make that same journey, down those same facts, to the conclusion that your client is not guilty.

Because some clients have a reason to selectively remember facts, try, at the early stage, to avoid allowing your client to add anything to your understanding about the case. The client's time to speak will come and your client may fill holes in your understanding with truth and useful insight. But that same client may inject wish and fantasy into the process. Wish and fantasy will distract you from your focus. You will give your client a chance to speak, but, best for you, not just yet.

If the client balks at being asked to remain silent, return to the poker playing analogy. Ask, how would you like to play high stakes poker for real money where you could see everyone else's cards before you had to place your bet? Your client will agree that would be nice. Explain that style of play is how you are running their case. Don't you want the upper hand in the game? Remind the client that the stakes are not money but freedom.

If, in your handling of the case, your client asserts that something is a fact, then it is a fact. You are stuck with it. Holding off the client's version of reality until YOU CAN TELL THE CLIENT THE

WHOLE STORY OF WHAT HE IS UP AGAINST helps your client not freelance with the facts. Freelancing can be a problem.

Set out the story you think the jury will accept from the facts as they are known to you. At this juncture don't worry about making your client guilty or not guilty. Get the story the jury will accept. Do all this, without the client's take on things, and you can see the case at the close of State's evidence. Is that story, standing alone, enough to convict your client? BE FAIR.

Remember the general rule – if the uncontroverted facts walk your client to guilty, in any way, shape or form, then there is a problem. The chasm in the evidence, identified by an overly forgiving defense counsel, is no more than a pebble in the path to the jury. Facts that get even close to guilty are a problem.

BUT IF, on just what you have, you have a strong presentation for reasonable doubt, or, even better, what looks like a clear "not guilty," then start teaching your theory of the case to your prosecutor.

If you have built your case analysis using your adversary's evidence, and if that evidence wins your case, go ahead and win the case. It may well be that once you have enumerated your uncontroverted facts, and articulated your issue, your theory of the case allows you to travel, without hesitation or pause, from the status of "accused" to "acquitted." When you can do this, AND when you are sure of your facts and conclusions, start pestering your prosecutor with what you have created. If, indeed, you have the facts correct, then the prosecutor will arrive at that same place. This is the zealous advocacy your client is seeking. Move things along. Get your client out from under. This is how most defense wins come. Not with an audience in a courtroom, but with a dismissal quietly filed in a clerks' office.

Articulating the issue helps frame the theory of the case. Articulating the theory helps you understand how to frame the issue. The words you ultimately choose to use are critical to finding your way to success. Some lawyers avoid this step in case preparation. They rely instead on a flurry of testimony and an argument that it all must add up to something – guilt/innocence/whatever. That will pass for a theory of the case, but it is weak.

It is better to (1) list your uncontroverted "true facts" and then (2) frame the issue of the case as a question, and (3) articulate a short story that is your theory of the case.

It may take some time for an articulable theory to emerge from the mush of facts. Don't worry about that. As you distinguish what is, and what is not, an uncontroverted fact you will start to see the "hole" that is the issue come into focus. As the issue becomes sharper how it works with the list of facts takes shape, and your short story, your theory seems to have been there the whole time. Remember that the *theory of the case* is a short story that:

Encompasses all the evidence, and
Explains and frames the issue, and
Demonstrates the fact that your side should win.

Until now your work has been investigation and diligence. Now you finally reach advocacy. It is common for your theory to deliver you to a threshold where you can, with authority, argue reasonable doubt. Most cases have holes. The theory of the case approach makes those holes stand out. You are working with a theory that is crafted from the other side's evidence. That is going to make it hard for the other side to deny what you say. You still have not asked your client a thing about his case.

In our example, we know that our jury is looking for a second shooter. Of the people who are without-a-doubt present at that crime scene at the relevant time, who might be the second shooter? Look back -- it is NOT an uncontroverted fact that the client is present. What does the other side's evidence say about where our client is when the shots are fired?

In our example we know the client's presence is in question. IF a juror even believes he is present, what evidence is there that your client is the second shooter? Having identified the issue you now look for a way to argue INCORPORATING THE UNCONTROVERTED FACTS that there is no evidence demonstrating that your client is the second shooter. Having made that argument, and not wishing to leave loose ends, you want to name that second shooter. Look over the list of who is there and pick your best candidate. How about the person the gun wielding 300 pound man was fighting? He is a state's witness, so he will be hard for the State to depend on him if we can impeach him. Might he be someone who would carry a gun?

In this scenario, with this State's witness on cross, you don't ask one single question about guns. If he will, let him brag and act innocent. Have other witnesses discuss who your second-shooter-candidate is as a person. After all, a man with a gun is looking for this fellow. Just who might he be? Will any witnesses make him out a bad guy? Bad guys might have guns. You know for certain that, in this case, there is a second weapon. Set your questions up so that, in closing, you can argue the state's witness is that second gunman.

Having a theory that (1) incorporates the uncontroverted facts, and then (2) addresses the issue in the case, and (3) explains how the evidence raises reasonable doubt about the client's guilt, or, even better, proves they are not guilty, gives you a framework in which to discuss the facts of what happened. Your jury, in deliberations, will try and piece together what occurred. From the story they assemble they will determine guilt. You have already done this work for the jury. Will they accept your take on the case? The simple theory which you teach your jury makes this possible. From voir dire through closing argument you keep chanting your theory of the case, like a mantra, over-and-over.

Take care to distinguish between facts and allegations. That can be a powerful distinction that gets lost on jurors. Most cases start with a few facts and piles of unsubstantiated and unproven allegations. This is especially true in the early hours of your involvement in the case. Once you have boiled the case down to the uncontroverted facts, supported by competent evidence and believable to a jury, most cases get easier to manage, at least in your own head. Uncontroverted facts may start as someone's allegation. Some allegations do turn out to be true facts. You must learn how to tell which is which.

This approach demonstrates a principle called "judo law." In the sport of judo one fighter seeks victory by using the other fighter's efforts against him. This is the same thing you are trying to do. In *theory of the case* you co-opt as much of the opponent's best moves (his evidence) and use them against him. Use HIS evidence to tell YOUR story. The other attorney may not even grasp what you are doing. So what if they do? They still have the burden of putting on their case, so what can they do? They must use their evidence to put on their case.

So, armed with your list, your issue and your first-generation theory of the case, stop and ask,

"WHERE AM I NOW?"

YOUR THEORY OF THE CASE SHOWS YOUR CLIENT WILL PREVAIL; AND YOUR THEORY IS BULLET PROOF. Really? If so, go bug your prosecutor. Maybe a lot, till they pay attention. Present this as a way your D.A. can mark another case "closed." That's what they want.

BUT,

WHAT IF YOUR THEORY POINTS TO GUILT?

Your theory will improve. After all, it's not a real theory until you win (in your theory). But let's be frank. Lots of clients are guilty. There may well be competent, admissible evidence of that fact. What seems simple to you is likely lost on your client. It will not be lost on the jury. If this is where you find yourself, you stand at a crossroads.

EITHER . . .

THE CLIENT ACCEPTS THAT THE FACTS GET HIM. He is realistic and mature about his situation. Work out the best plea you can. Perhaps your client will accept it. That decision is his/hers. This is the crossroads – the choice between trial and the best plea we are going to get – where due diligence delivers you. Now, it is your client who faces the hard choice between two unhappy alternatives. Your client will ask what they should do.

This is where you find out just how much, if at all, the client trusts you. Will they believe in what you advise? Will they face a bad situation and mitigate their damages? Will they roll the dice?

OR . . .

Clients commonly DO NOT, AND WILL NOT, ACCEPT THE STORY told by the facts of their case. Such a client is going to trial, even with no realistic chance to prevail. When this is where you find yourself:

First, shift into full CYA mode. Every act and consideration on your part gets a memo to the file. Your client gets lots of letters documenting these decisions. Create, in those letters and memos, a paper trail showing where you have been, where you are, and where you might be going. Explain why you have decided what you have decided. If, as is probable, sometime in the future you have to explain to some reviewing authority why you did what you did, this level of detail will help refresh your memory. Any critiquing will not occur for some years down the road. With this level of detail in the file you will have the information you will need to explain what you did.

Next, start prepping for trial. Honor your list of uncontroverted facts. They must not be denied. Your theory of the case may show you the need to shift the focus of your trial from "what" happened to "why" it happened. There are situations where getting your client's entire story out in the open may be the best tactic available. If the issue at trial is as simple as "did my guy do it?" you may get fast tracked to a guilty verdict. If you can make the trial be about why this happened you may find some room to maneuver. If guilty is inevitable, make the question "guilty of what?" Remember that many cases are resolved for less than one side wants but more than the other side hoped to lose.

Nothing is ever open-and-shut unless you let it be.

You may have little to work with in any particular case. You can always sit back and snipe at the other side's case. Watch and see if your opponents deny any of the uncontroverted facts. If they do, point this out to your jury. Show your jury that they disagree with your adversary.

Watch to see that, IF you revealed your theory of the case in your opening statement, is the other side rushing to respond to your story? Or are they maintaining their own case and putting on their story without concern for you? Use this to judge how confident they are in their story.

I say "if" you revealed your theory in opening. Perhaps you have reserved your opening statement for your part of the case. This can be done to give your adversary as little notice as possible of what you are thinking. Now, when it is your time to do opening statement you skip it and go right to your first witness. After all, this deep in, with one side done presenting their evidence, no one in the courtroom is thinking about an opening statement. The only time the jury will hear your theory intact is in your closing statement. This should leave the other side with no time to find and develop any rebuttal evidence. There may be times such a ploy will work. Such decision must be made on a case-by-case basis, but can be "gamed" out ahead of time without obligating counsel to follow any particular track.

The question becomes, what do you have to put in? What can you do to affirmatively carry your case? Many lawyers come out of law school believing they can just sit back and kvetch that the other side has not proved their case. That might work if what's left unproved are essential elements of the prima facie case. It's okay to kvetch if what is missing is essential and material. But if you are arguing about the color shirt your client is wearing, and there is no real dispute that it's your client in the shirt, then your theory needs more work.

One side or the other must convince the jury of something. If one side comes forward with something, the jury tends to think that is the case. If you merely argue that the other side has failed to carry its' burden, the jury may decide that "something" weighs more than your complaints. Something always beats nothing.

NEXT HERESY

Which brings up our next heresy – the presumption of innocence. Judges tell the jury about the presumption and make a big deal out of it. Don't you believe it. To your jury the fact that your client is charged at all means *he is guilty of something*. You have to show the jury someway, somehow, that your client is not guilty. That is what you are doing at trial. Nothing else.

Law school provides a head full of "presumption of innocence." The judge is happy to instruct your jury about what that is and what it means. Don't rest your case here. The presumption that the jury thinks your client is innocent is a dangerous myth. Avoid its' siren song. Your jury believes in the presumption of innocence, just not for your client, who is, after all, on trial.

For jurors, *your client is guilty of something* or he would not be a defendant. Why else would we be having a trial? Counsel should work from the presumption of GUILTY IF CHARGED. Guilty if charged is a lot closer to how things really work than is the presumption of innocence. Don't pretend it's otherwise. Accept that you have a burden to demonstrate that your client is not guilty if you want any chance of winning that verdict from a jury.

I believe the jury wants to hear the Defendant, who has pled "not guilty," get on the witness stand and say, "not guilty." Clients have a million reasons for not wanting to take the stand. But this is so central – are you guilty? –I tell my client that if we go to trial they should expect to take the stand on their own behalf. Things often don't work out that way, but this is our starting point.

PUTTING ON A CASE

Keep your focus on presenting your story through your theory of the case. As much as you can, use the other side's evidence to tell your story. Do not just sit back and complain about the other side's shortcomings. This is seldom sufficient to carry the day.

When addressing the question of what part(s) of the case you must put on, you return to the *theory of the case*. How much of your theory has been told by the other side's evidence? Whatever part of your theory has not been proved by the other party's evidence is what *you must put into evidence*. Your goal of teaching the jury your theory has not changed. Calculate if your complete theory is in evidence. Once it is you can stop presenting evidence. Do you have in evidence the information you need to make your closing argument?

On a sheet of paper break your theory down into its various clauses. See how a shorter theory is easier? Make a chart showing which witness provides which information. Make a check-off column for tracking their testimony at trial. Make notes on questions you can ask each witness to flesh out the part(s) of the story they have that you want. Identify which witness gets each clause of your theory into evidence. Understanding this is your responsibility. As any witness takes the stand you already know what they are going to do for you. This allows you to remain polite and courteous with the witness, something that jurors like. Should you ever decide to rough up a witness, be sure you can articulate why. Then make sure the jury understands "why." Being mean or rude for the sake of being mean or rude is seldom useful. Same goes for being snarky.

When an opposing witness is giving part of your story, be nice to that witness. You can be fairly certain they expect you to be an ass, so don't. The witness is unlikely to grasp that they are helping to sell your theory of the case. Why be anything but gracious to any witness who is helping your efforts? And, since you are being nice, there is a good chance the witness will be nice to you. It's hard to be rude to a polite person. This will help manage your stress level.

If you ever have a witness get rude with you, especially if that witness is working against your position, let them be as rude as they wish. Respond to their rudeness with ever increasing politeness and courtesy. Generally, people don't like rudeness, and there are people on your jury.

Identify which parts of your theory have gotten to the jury and where holes remain. If you want to argue something in closing you must get the idea into evidence. At close of state's evidence you can argue that your theory-identified holes in their case represent essential elements of the crime charged. This gives you an argument for dismissal.

Always point out how your case is made by the other side's evidence. This is strong. Set your opponent up, potentially, to argue against the very evidence he put in. I sure hope he tries.

You may identify parts of the theory / story for which you will have to provide evidence. Consider whether to get this information through the client or someone else. The algebra of whether the client takes the stand is for them to complete, but I always tell clients that if they are not guilty the jury wants them to take the stand and say so. In the jury *group mind* is the thought that, "if you are not guilty, why don't you say so yourself?" We know there are many reasons why the client may not, or will not, take the stand. It may be another heresy, but I set the expectation with my client that, at trial, the client takes the stand.

The case which gets presented to the jury is the same whether or not you put on evidence. Your purpose is to sell the jury on the idea that your theory of the case is the way to understand this mess. Using a theory which is short and concise allows that theory to be taught to your jury in a few minutes / hours of time. Simpler is better, as long as your whole theory gets in play. Remember that theory must:

(1) Explain the evidence, and
(2) Frame the issue, and
(3) Demonstrate why your client is in the right

This is a manageable task when you have understood the uncontroverted facts of the case, see how those facts frame your issue, and can explain why you win.

Theory of the case allows you to know which witness gives you what. This technique will illuminate problems if they exist. Be willing to see what is there.

WHEN YOUR CLIENT IS THE ONE TELLING THE TRUTH

There is an interesting position that does happen from time to time. After collecting your uncontroverted facts and identifying the issue you find yourself with questions left unanswered by the other side's evidence. It is finally time to hear the client's side of the story. Ask your client *SPECIFIC QUESTIONS ADDRESSED TO THOSE GAPS IN THE STORY.* Your client will be confused as to why, after all this time, you want his story at all.

Consider this as a tactical problem. There is a gap in the story the other side cannot fill. It turns out that your client can bridge that gap. Only you can put your client on the stand, so, should you do so? First, test how vital that gap is by making it the centerpiece of a Motion to Dismiss at close of State's evidence. If the motion carries, you go home. If the motion fails you can put the client up or not. Renew the same argument in closing after you rest.

Whatever is missing becomes the "great unknown." What will be important is whether your client has facts that are relevant to the "great unknown." If your client can bring light to an unresolved issue, that may be the way to go. Or, it may be that the facts your client adds do not help sell your theory of the case. But if the client hooks up important parts of your theory, be open to the possibility of the client's testimony carrying the case.

THEORY OF THE CASE AND TRIAL PRACTICE

Everything you do, from voir dire to closing, is about selling your theory to the jury. Teach your jury as much theory as any situation allows. With any State's witness there is always the question of whether or not to cross. This analysis is simple: can this witness "sell" any (or all) of your theory to the jury? If they can add something, let them. It is often possible to take something of value from each witness who is arguably there to hurt your case.

Work the truth of your theory. Do not panic and validate unsupported allegation from the other side. Teach your theory. Let opposing witnesses teach as much of your theory as possible. Don't lose sight of the fact that while you spent hundreds of hours reaching your understanding of the case, the jury must reach that same level in only a few minutes. They can do that if they adopt your theory of the case. Wave your flag every chance you get.

There is an old adage used in sales, called the K.I.S.S. formula. It stands for "Keep It Simple, Stupid." This is too true to ignore. Don't make your case more complicated, make it less. Make the story something the jury can follow. Your theory should make sense to both you and to the jury. Juries get bored. Move things along by knowing what you want to convey – your theory. If the jury agrees with you, you may do alright.

The theory is what decides if any particular witness gets questioned at all. If a witness can help you sell your theory, especially if this witness is called by the other side, develop that testimony. THEIR witness adds great gravitas to YOUR story. On the other hand, a witness who has not damaged your theory, but does not help your theory, can be dismissed. There is no reason or etiquette to question anyone simply because they are on the witness stand. There is some argument that speaking less at trial makes what you do say carry more weight. You can ask any question that advances acceptance of your theory by the jury. If the witness cannot help your efforts say, "No questions."

Importantly, do not allow a witness who has hurt you to repeat their bad story a second or third time. Pretend a witness has hurt your theory, and you are not sure you can fix what they did. If you take them on cross, at a minimum they will get a second chance to give their version. Then the State gets re-direct and the witness gets to tell their bad tale a third time. Will you re-cross and let them go for five on re-re-direct? One bad story told once or one bad story told how many times? If the witness did not help sell your theory, consider minimizing the damage and say, "no questions."

When you finally reach closing arguments, once again sell your theory and stress how the other side's evidence shows you are right.

LATE-ARRIVING EVIDENCE

A perpetual problem with trial practice is late-arriving evidence. This may be intentional with an unethical opponent, or it may reflect the volume of information they are trying to get delivered to you. Maybe they are trying to squeeze you for a continuance. It happens. If you have an articulable theory late arriving evidence is a manageable problem. Your theory takes the pressure out of this all-too-common eventuality.

Smile as you receive the late arriving package from the State. You may as well smile as you know the judge will not give you any delay in starting the trial. Your first question is, *does this late arriving evidence require a change to my list of uncontroverted facts?* This is your first concern. If your uncontroverted facts change everything might change. Determine if anything needs to be adjusted.

Seldom does late arriving evidence do much more than prove duplicative of what you already know. In many cases this late arriving information is irrelevant to your theory and does not impact what you plan to do. You will be able to proceed as planned.

If the late arriving evidence does contradict an uncontroverted fact, question which of the two is correct? Make what adjustments are necessary and watch to see if opposing counsel catches the change. Is your issue impacted? Always watch for your opponent to contradict something your jury thinks is true. Watch to see if the side offering the late arriving evidence is enamored with that evidence. You can just tell they want to use it, so they will. If you just know it's coming, how can you use it?

Return to the premise of JUDO LAW – using your opponent's efforts against him. If you get lucky and your legal adversary for some reason is blinded by his late arriving information, he or she may fail to see how the entire puzzle fits together. Watch for your opponent to deny the truth of the uncontroverted facts.

An articulated theory allows you to subject late arriving evidence to the same analysis as all the other evidence. Does this information help me sell my theory to my jury? If the late arriving evidence is useful, add it to your quiver. If it is not helpful to you, BUT does not require you to reassess your work, it is not important enough to upset your applecart at this late hour.

# # #

THE FORMULA

To craft a theory of the case become intimately familiar with the uncontroverted facts of your case. These facts are, for the purposes of this case, true for your jury and true for you. Every chance you get to acknowledge this list to your jury -- to say something true to your jury – take it.

Once you know the bedrock facts of your case, start walking those facts with the question of why your client is in trouble. You are looking for the hole, the error, the mistake in the case that has brought your client to this sorry state. You just might see the bit of evidence that makes your client guilty. This is your issue of the case.

Finally, using your uncontroverted facts (as they come through the other side's presentation of evidence), explain why your client is not guilty of what he is charged. If you can do this in 100 words, that is good; 50 words are better; 25 would be golden. Remember, these are the words you need your jury to accept if you are to prevail.

A Quick Word on Frustration

I can't remember anyone in law school ever mentioning that any client of mine might actually be guilty of his charges. That's something that might be useful to know. Fortunately it is taught in the school of hard knocks.

The practice of law is a toxic occupation. It hurts and damages those who practice, even those who deny or don't appreciate what is happening to them. Lawyers roll around in the worst things people can do, and do do, to each other. Eventually a bit of that nastiness sticks, gets inside, and turns people mean. You may already have seen this happen to someone you know.

Doctors, to survive their occupation, develop a bedside manner that is comforting but a bit distant. You must be supportive of your client and not get sucked into the chaos of their life. That's the balancing act all lawyers attempt. If you master this vital skill please share what you understand.

So drink coffee with your colleagues, not your clients. Once in a while slip away to a movie in the afternoon. Take a vacation. It's important work and we need you credible while doing it.

AFTERWORD

Theory of the case teaches you to understand your case the way your jury will. You do not want to go chasing bits of information in huge files while the jury sits and wonders how you ever passed the bar exam. Using theory of the case helps you grasp what your client is up against and what you need to show to carry the day. It is a short and hopefully simple story that you are calm and comfortable discussing with your jury.

It is all about your credibility before the jury.[1]

# # #

[1] Did you think you had read an entire book about law without one footnote?

- NOTES -

Printed in Dunstable, United Kingdom

91219608R00051